Open Cabinets

Habeeba Ahmed

BookLeaf
Publishing

India | USA | UK

Presentation by *BookLeaf Publishing*

Web: www.bookleafpub.com

E-mail: info@bookleafpub.com

ISBN: 9789358319606

First edition 2023

Words, words, words

Sometimes
I can't,
               find the   right words.
the good
words
the generous ones.

when I say hi, I really mean
hello when I say bye
I mean don't go
just yet   when I
say I missed you I mean
you were with me always!!!! So how can a
time come
when the words I say aren't for you?

I can't say this.
Yes, I can't say this.

Love and Symbiosis

I sit here disillusioned, yet in wait of course.
I am alive I say, but it's all-in haste of course.
I belong now to this land,
where the water seems earnest,
but never quite meets the sand.
a land, where the mountains are unpegged.
Where the sky cries and cries, but the ground
dries up instead.
And I wondered at this ground,
why it mocks at its lover?
why it dies for the likes of this?
Why it chooses to suffer?
But then I knowingly muttered,
that the sky cries to kiss the ground,
but the ground dies so as to not be drowned.
Both will do as they will, and both will do as
they should.

But isn't love, just another way to wait?
Another way to remain still.

Was is love?
if not symbiosis?

Herself

there's a whole story encapsulated within his
name is what she tried to tell them.
you mean the meaning of his name is beautiful?
No, she quipped with an impatience that seemed
misplaced.

His name had represented something eternal --
some theme that had existed since the beginning.
You see, when she'd speak his name, she'd feel
more like herself. if she had known these words
and if they had lived in her for a time, she'd
simply say it. she feels less strange, is what she
said. But she meant that she felt more like
herself and less like him.

she said, I can move all smooth between time
and space. that I felt fuzzy and strange and
ill-defined my whole life, moving around like a
formless cloud. but when I speak his name, I
was beaming. And she was -- she was. Still
unable to be grasped yes, but there, right there,
can you see it? Of course, you do.

When I say his name, I feel more like myself
and less like him.

That's what she meant to say,
That's what she meant.

Stingy

I'm grateful for this heart,
That hurts this way.
That wants for nothing,
but to leave its own mold.
A heart so
reluctant.
that it hides itself.
it hides itself; it hides itself.

Land of Eternal Love

in sheer innocence,
I'd wonder
at where love would hide.

much like Abraham,
I would point to the
jewels
hanging from the sky,
asking
Is this what I'm meant to love?

and when each would set and rise,
as such things do
I'd grow tired

lamenting that
I would
be left to wander
once again.

but now,
I see true love as a thing that doesn't hide.
as ever-present,
needing not
to be captured or

shrouded in petty disguise.
love is pure.
Yes, love is pure.
simply because it originates
from the source
of all purity.
so may His love continue to reach us,
embrace us,
and carry us,
until we return
to the final home.
where rivers flow,

to the land
where eternal love lives

and where it grows
and grows
and grows.

Untitled

I began in witness. I began as a witness, of your
power and might and subtlety
And I now find myselfin an awethat
predates my body.

I'm lostin primordial awe.

and in this moment,my mind returns to youin
submissionjust as my soul will.

Glorified are you.

Some advice

surround yourself with the kind.

with the earnest.

with the open-hearted.

such that you feel yourself grow earnest in their company.

to feel with those who feel.

with those who choose a good word, an uplifting word, a kind word.

who feel like fresh air.

who feel like fresh air.

who feel like fresh air.

Hope

I still wonder
about you, wondering
if you still wander
in that lost way
that you do. are you happy have you eaten, do
you still get that
excited on
the phone,
without ever
trying, and always hiding
so as to not let
your loneliness, show
                I always hope you're happy.

I really do. I hope you learn
to step outside of yourself soon.
I hope you learn to love
yourself the way you're
meant to. and somehow learn to
never bite the hand that
feeds you.
I hope I hope

Trans Canada

I want you to come toward
me as I come toward you,
I saw the trans Canada
sign,
and felt my heart
sigh
because I thought of you
friendship lost, a lover unwilling,
to whom do I complain
to whom do I owe apology.
Do you think of me,
as I think of you? do you reminisce and miss me,
as I do you.
you were always coming toward me,
but never I toward you. I'm sorry I
thought so little of you. and now I long and
extend my arm out, to no one really. to no one
ever.

I miss you

I miss you
as the days grow warmer
and the cherries start to swoon
I miss you
not during those cold still nights
but when i too start to bloom
I miss you
not when I forget my own name
not when the sweet sound of your sigh
starts to wade
and not even as I awaken to your face
as it fades
I miss you
not knowing how or why or when
not missing you as I cry
but as I laugh
as my heart moves and as it spins
I miss you.

in the good times,
not the bad

                    i miss you.
in the good times,
never the bad.

A Little Leaf

lifelessly
falling from the tree
it met the ground.
only to be swept up by
violent winds that do
with it as they please

and you can
say what you will
about the passive leaf
but it's Lord knows.
when it falls, when it drifts, where it sits
He knows it

and because
it too is enveloped
in His knowledge,
maybe the little leaf
has a home
in Him
too

Lost Keys

I seem to
lose and find myself
like one loses and finds
a pair of keys.

but
even in
the confusing depths
of this wayward
bloom,

I tell myself,

that all self knowledge
is derived
from knowing You.

such that
when I find You, my Lord
I'll find me too.

yes.
I'll find me too.

the moon was patient

the moon was patient,
it would glisten for me
even while shrouded by clouds.

it would emulate
the brilliance of the sun
though it contained no light itself.

like a lighthouse,

it would guide
the dark
tumultuous sea.

and in spite of everything,

the moon was always you,
and the lost one was me.

To my nafs

I'm sorry my dear,
for not trying to
understand you.

I should've
approached you
from a place
of compassion,

from a place of mercy.

I should've taken your hand,
in mine, and
asked to make amends.

— an open conversation with my nafs

Untitled 2

maybe this burning,
has some life,
too.

maybe this standing,
on the edge,
has a purpose,
too.

Sweet Nothings

to be in constant motion,
is to move
while longing to be still.

it's to feel the restless
turning of your heart,
coming and going
coming and going,

it's to feel foreign.

my dear,
since meeting you,
I don't know of
any other way of being
in this world,
except for this.

Frail Bird

oh frail little bird,
that chirps incessantly at my window,
I'd grown tired of you,
loathing your sharpness

but I seek now
to understand you,
to come to know you,

as a being
that chirps in remembrance

oh frail little bird,
I hope you find what you're seeking.
and the one that you're seeking.

and I hope that I learn
to sleep knowingly
and sombrely,
while you exist in this world,
in the only way that you know how

Questions

what do you do,
when your feelings
feel more
like questions
that incessantly
prod you for
answers

and what do I do
now that I
look to you
to answer
my heart's questions

what do I do with me
and what do I do with you

(and isn't it funny that even
in these matters
I still ask you)

Unassuming

the soft,
unassuming one,

often enters this world
adrift.

but they
must come to know

that they have
their heart
as a compass

gifted to them
by their Lord.

a Conversation

أَتَىٰ أَمْرُ اللَّهِ فَلَا تَسْتَعْجِلُوهُ

my Lord comforts me in words,
and I respond with feelings
that cant seem to find
no language
to speak in.
سُبْحَانَهُ وَتَعَالَىٰ عَمَّا يُشْرِكُون

my Lord comforts me in words,
and my heart
glorifies Him with feelings
that can't seem to
find no mode
of expression.

but my Lord understands me.
He tells my heart to be still.

and so I sit here,
with a spinning heart
and a mind
lost in a trance,

waiting silently,
for the promise of my Lord.

New Feelings

New feelings seem
to arrive without warning
like rude guests
and I of course invite them in.
I even sit with them and listen as they speak in
garbled words that carry no meaning.

but today was a bit different.
today she said, after lying down on my couch,
that my longing is dissipating.
yes, my longing is dissipating.
"just like you wanted"

but I pointed to the weight on my chest and I
asked
"what's this then?"
and she smiled knowingly
"well my dear,
they lived there
so what do you think happens when someone
who occupies a space leaves it?
You feel their absence."
"But shouldn't I feel emptiness instead ?"
She smiled knowingly again.

"my dear, a love that is earnest doesn't dissipate
after the person departs.
what you feel is their memory living inside of
you, growing and changing everyday.
Oh no I thought. I'm ruined I thought.
but her voice was comforting,
"Oh don't lament my dear, that's simply
wonderful.
It shows
that you keep your memories alive ... and
how beautiful is that?"
and just then,
She drank all of my lemon tea,
Gathered all of her belongings
And left without looking back.

how rude, I wondered
But I too smiled a small smile,
in gratitude perhaps,
For being able to learn
from such fickle feelings.